11.95

DUE DATE

THE IRISH POTATO FAMINE

by
Don Nardo

Illustrations by
Brian McGovern

LUCENT
B·O·O·K·S

WORLD DISASTERS

These and other titles are available in the Lucent World Disasters Series:

The Armenian Earthquake	**The Ethiopian Famine**
The Bhopal Chemical Leak	**The Hindenburg**
The Black Death	**Hiroshima**
The Challenger	**The Irish Potato Famine**
Chernobyl	**Krakatoa**
The Chicago Fire	**Pompeii**
The Crash of 1929	**The San Francisco Earthquake**
The Dust Bowl	**The Titanic**

Library of Congress Cataloging-in-Publication Data

Nardo, Don, 1947-
      The Irish potato famine / by Don Nardo ; illustrations by Brian McGovern
      p. cm. — (World disasters)
      Includes bibliographical references.
      Summary: Examines the historical, economic, scientific, and human factors involved in the great famine in Ireland in the nineteenth century
      ISBN 1-56006-012-3
      1. Famines—Ireland—History—19th century—Juvenile literature.
2. Ireland—Economic conditions—Juvenile literature. 3. Famines—Juvenile literature. [1. Famines—Ireland—History—19th century.] I. McGovern, Brian, ill. II. Title. III. Series.
HC260.5.Z9F36 1990
363.8'09415'09034—dc20   90-6246
                                                                        CIP
                                                                        AC

© Copyright 1990 by Lucent Books, Inc.
Lucent Books, Inc., P.O. Box 289011, San Diego, California, 92198-0011

*To Bonnie Szumski whose talent and skill
helped shape this work.*

Table of Contents

Preface: The World Disasters Series 5

Introduction: Ireland's Great Hunger.................6

One: Early Ireland—A Legacy of British Influence 8

Two: A Land Poised on the Brink of Ruin 20

Three: A Deadly Blight Brings National Tragedy 30

Four: Death and Flight—Ireland Depopulated 46

Five: World Hunger—Famine Still Plagues Humanity 52

Glossary.....................................60

Works Consulted......................61

Index 62

Picture Credits 63

About the Author and Illustrator ...64

Preface
The World Disasters Series

World disasters have always aroused human curiosity. Whenever news of tragedy spreads, we want to learn more about it. We wonder how and why the disaster happened, how people reacted, and whether we might have acted differently. To be sure, disaster evokes a wide range of responses—fear, sorrow, despair, generosity, even hope. Yet from every great disaster, one remarkable truth always seems to emerge: in spite of death, pain, and destruction, the human spirit triumphs.

History is full of disasters, arising from a variety of causes. Earthquakes, floods, volcanic eruptions, and other natural events often produce widespread destruction. Just as often, however, people accidentally bring suffering and distress on themselves and other human beings. And many disasters have sinister causes, like human greed, envy, or prejudice.

The disasters included in this series have been chosen not only for their dramatic qualities, but also for their educational value. The reader will learn about the causes and effects of the greatest disasters in history. Technical concepts and interesting anecdotes are explained and illustrated in inset boxes.

But disasters should not be viewed in isolation. To enrich the reader's understanding, these books present historical information about the time period, and interesting facts about the culture in which each disaster occurred. Finally, they teach valuable lessons about human nature. More acts of bravery, cowardice, intelligence, and foolishness are compressed into the few days of a disaster than most people experience in a lifetime.

Dramatic illustrations and evocative narrative lure the reader to distant cities and times gone by. Readers witness the awesome power of an exploding volcano, the magnitude of a violent earthquake, and the hopelessness of passengers on a mighty ship passing to its watery grave. By reliving the events, the reader will see how disaster affects the lives of real people and will gain a deeper understanding of their sorrow, their pain, their courage, and their hope.

Introduction

Ireland's Great Hunger

In 1840, there were more than eight million people living in Ireland, an island about the size of the state of West Virginia. Most were poor farmers who could not afford to own their own land. They raised crops of wheat and barley, which they used instead of money to pay rent to their rich landlords, many of whom lived across the Irish Sea in England. To ensure that there would always be enough crops to pay the rent, the Irish peasants almost never ate the grains they grew. Instead, they lived almost exclusively on a diet of potatoes.

In 1845, a terrible blight, or disease, hit the Irish potato crop. The potatoes rotted in the fields, releasing a sickening stench across the countryside. People tried everything they could think of to combat the disease. They boiled the potatoes and treated them with salt. They soaked them in bog water and exposed them to poisonous gas.

The Irish Potato Famine in History

400 B.C.
Celts invade and conquer Ireland

432
St. Patrick converts Ireland to Christianity

795
Vikings invade and conquer Ireland

800
Irish monks produce the *Book of Kells*

1014
Irish King Brian Boru expels Vikings from Ireland

1171
King Henry II of England claims rulership of Ireland

1530
Spaniards bring potatoes to Europe from South America

1534
English Church separates from Roman Catholic Church; persecution of Irish Catholics begins

1688
Irish-supported Glorious Revolution replaces Catholic King James of England with Protestant King William

1798
First Irish rebellion against Britain fails

1801
Act of Union makes Ireland part of Great Britain

1841
Robert Peel elected British Prime Minister

1845
Blight destroys Ireland's potato crop; famine begins

1846
British Corn Laws repealed

1847-1854
1,600,000 Irish emigrate to the U.S.

1854
Violent anti-Irish demonstrations in U.S. cities

1876
Great famine of China

1914
World War I begins

But nothing worked. The blight quickly swept across the island and people starved by the thousands.

Since thousands of poor farmers had to eat their cash crops, they could no longer pay their rent, so their landlords evicted them. Homeless families had no money and few job skills beyond a rudimentary knowledge of farming. Unable to find work or decent shelter, tens of thousands of homeless people languished in caves and ditches. There, many slowly became weak from hunger and disease and finally died.

The potatoes continued to rot in the fields each year until 1850. The resulting famine was a national disaster for the Irish. The great hunger killed entire families. Villages stood abandoned, and dead bodies littered fields and roadsides. One witness described how "they hauled the bodies in wagons and laid them in pits. There was no money for coffins nor strength to dig separate graves."

In all, more than one million Irish died of starvation or hunger-related diseases in the great potato famine. Millions more fled the country. The potato crop eventually recovered, but the country did not. It took many years for the Irish to repair the economic and social damages caused by the famine. And even after many generations, the Irish have not forgotten the ordeal their ancestors suffered. The terrible memory of the hunger lingers, a legacy of the catastrophe of the 1840s.

1916
Irish revolt against British, known as the Easter Rebellion, fails

1919
Rebel remnants of Easter Rebellion form the Irish Republican Army (IRA), an anti-British terrorist organization

1921
Great famine of Russia

1922
Ireland divided into Irish Free State and Northern Ireland

1937
New constitution adopted; country's official name becomes Eire

1939
World War II begins

1949
Ireland withdraws from British Commonwealth; becomes Republic of Ireland

1955
Ireland joins the United Nations

1958
Major outbreak of potato blight in Ireland

1960
John F. Kennedy becomes first Irish-American Catholic U.S. president

1962
IRA (Irish Republican Army) leaders declare cease-fire on terrorist activities.

1962
IRA splits into socialist and terrorist factions; terrorism resumes

1985
Great famine of Ethiopia

1987
Unemployment in Ireland reaches 18 percent

One

Early Ireland—A Legacy of British Influence

Ireland is an island located west of the larger island of Great Britain. Separated from Britain by a channel known as the Irish Sea, Ireland is about 110 miles wide, and 220 miles long and occupies an area of about 32,600 square miles. The island is divided into two parts—the Republic of Ireland and Northern Ireland. The official creation of two separate Irish states occurred in 1921, at which time Britain gave up its control of most of the territory of Ireland and allowed the Republic to become an independent country. Northern Ireland remains a part of Great Britain. Together, Northern Ireland and Great Britain constitute the United Kingdom.

Because of Ireland's proximity to Britain, British culture, politics, and religion have significantly influenced the Irish since ancient times. For instance, Ireland's earliest inhabitants, the Celts, migrated to Britain in the fifth century B.C. The Celts made their living by farming and raising livestock. They were also skilled metalworkers who worked with copper, bronze, and gold. From these metals, they produced useful items such as tools, bowls, and drinking cups, as well as ornamental jewelry and hunting horns. Later, Celtic artisans learned to use iron and fashion it into knives, swords, shields, and spearheads.

The Celts were polytheistic which means that they worshipped many gods. The most important was Danu, the mother goddess who made sure the crops grew and that domestic animals multiplied. There were also less powerful, local gods who protected individual tribes and villages. The religious leaders, called druids, held positions of great power and respect in Celtic communities. The druids, who were poets as well as priests, claimed to have great knowledge of the gods, the afterlife, and the future.

Many Kingdoms

There were many separate Celtic kingdoms, or *tuaths*, and each tuath had a king, or *ri*. Some of the most powerful of these early kingdoms were called Ulster, Meath, and Connaught. Later, these became the names of Irish counties. The kingdoms continually fought one

A page from the *Book of Kells* from the Trinity College Library in Dublin, Ireland.
The art of manuscript illumination is particularly evident in this beautiful work.

WHERE IS IRELAND?

Ireland consists of two parts, the Republic of Ireland and Northern Ireland. It is located west of Great Britain, which is made up of England, Wales, and Scotland. Ireland and Great Britain are separated by the Irish Sea, a small channel that averages fifty to one hundred miles in width.

IRELAND
Dublin •

GREAT
BRITAIN

London •

FRANCE

Atlantic
Ocean

another for control of the Irish countryside.

About A.D. 432, Celtic religion was drastically changed by a British Christian priest named Patrick. He sailed to Ireland and, in only a few years, converted most of the natives to Christianity. Later, he became known as Saint Patrick, whom many Irish Catholics still believe watches over and protects the Irish people.

Brought Latin Language

The new religion, overseen by the Roman Catholic Church, brought the Latin language to the people of Ireland, who discovered a need for churches and religious books. Irish priests and scholars decorated their religious texts with elaborate drawings and lettering, in an ancient artistic style known as illumination. The most famous of the Irish illuminated manuscripts is the *Book of Kells,* a beautifully illustrated version of four books from the Bible. The Irish also added elaborate decorations to the churches they constructed. In the first few Christian centuries in Ireland, the people built many beautiful monasteries and small chapels.

Although the Irish proved themselves devout Catholics, Ireland was far from Rome and contacts between the two locales were infrequent. The pope, the leader of the church, found it difficult to administer church affairs over so great a distance and searched for ways to exercise more control over Ireland. Pope Adrian IV decided to gain such control by taking advantage of

THE ART OF IRISH MANUSCRIPT ILLUMINATION

Manuscript illumination is the application of artistic drawings, designs, and letterings to handwritten or printed books. Many ancient peoples, including the Egyptians, Greeks, and Romans, practiced illumination. But the art form reached its highest level of accomplishment in Ireland during the seventh and eighth centuries.

The Irish artists produced extremely intricate designs that often began around a single letter, then spread out to cover a whole page. The style of these designs developed from an earlier style of Celtic art that featured elaborate patterns of curves and spirals. Usually, Irish illuminators did not realistically depict objects or people. Instead, they worked such figures into the designs, making the objects and people difficult to pick out at first glance. The colors most commonly used by the Irish artists were gold, yellow, light blue, and deep red.

The first important Irish illuminated manuscript was the *Book of Durrow*, produced in about A.D. 700. The *Book of Kells* became the best-known example of this art form. Written by monks in the county of Kells in about 800, the book contains the four Gospels from the Bible. Later, Irish missionaries carried copies of these and other illuminated manuscripts to many parts of Europe.

This photograph taken from the *Book of Kells* shows the painstaking work that went into this beautiful, handmade book.

Ireland's nearness to Britain. He reasoned that he could better administer Ireland through the powerful English Catholic Church. In 1155, the pope granted "ownership" of Ireland to King Henry II of England. Henry landed an army at Waterford in southern Ireland in 1171 and quickly took control of the country. This was the beginning of more than seven centuries of British domination of Ireland.

The British began imposing heavy taxes on the Irish immediately. Most Irish were poor, and in order to pay these taxes they had to sell the best of their wheat, barley, and other grains to the British. What was left was often barely enough to live on. The best of Ireland's crops and livestock routinely ended up on British dinner tables. This unfair taxation, coupled with resentment over the British invasion, caused much hatred of the British in Ireland.

An Act of Treason

In the 1500s, Britain again influenced the fate of Ireland when England broke away from the Roman Catholic Church. King Henry VIII and English legislators passed laws recognizing the king, not the pope, as head of the English Church. Henry declared any opposition to his authority in church matters an act of treason and executed many people who defied the new laws. He also ordered the establishment of his new "Protestant" church in all the lands under his rule, including Ireland. The devout Irish Catholics strongly objected. The British re-

King Henry VIII executed many people who defied his laws recognizing the king, not the pope, as head of the English Church.

sponded harshly to these objections by instituting anti-Catholic "penal laws." Under these measures, Catholics could not hold public office nor attend Catholic mass, which was banned. In addition, the British banished most Catholic priests and forbade Catholics from running schools or carrying arms without a license. The enforcement of these penal laws during the 1500s and 1600s caused the Irish to hate the British more than ever.

While the British persecuted Irish Catholics, wealthy and powerful Britons seized lands from Irish farmers. After establishing their farms, these landlords went back to Britain. The landlords allowed poor Irish farmers to live on the land and to work it. These farmers were tenants and did not own any part of the land they farmed. On this land, the tenants could build small cottages to house their families. In return for this privilege, they had to ship nearly all the crops and livestock they raised to their British landlords. The rent crops and animals consisted of grains like wheat, barley, and hay and a few pigs and cattle. The tenant farmers almost never ate these items for fear they would not be able to pay their rent. Instead, they ate mostly potatoes, a sufficient amount of which could be grown on a small portion of an average farm. The milk and butter from the cows were the only substantial supplements to the potatoes in the diet of the poor. The Irish tenant farmers owned nothing and made

no profit from the sale of the crops. They had no chance to escape the poverty in which they lived. Most landlords employed agents, or Irish overseers, who kept track of the tenants and made sure the system ran smoothly.

If things did not run smoothly, or an Irish tenant farmer protested his lot, the British landlord could put a cruel practice into action. Under British law, landlords could evict, or throw out, tenants any time they wanted to. At the landlord's word, an agent could evict a family in less than an hour. The process of eviction, often called "tumbling," began when the agent, accompanied by the police, arrived at a tenant farmer's home. The farmer and his

Many landlords ruthlessly evicted Irish poor who could not pay their rent.

THE BLOODY UPRISING OF 1798

The rebellion of 1798 left a scar on the spirit of Irish independence. It made generations of Irish afraid to resist British oppression. This fear contributed to the feelings of dependence and helplessness that would later characterize the Irish peasants during times of great famine.

A secretary of the Catholic Committee, Theobald Wolfe Tone, published revolutionary pamphlets in the early 1790s. These urged all Irish to resist British oppression by whatever means necessary. Tone went to France in 1796 and convinced French leaders to help the Irish gain freedom. Later that year, a large French military expedition sailed for Ireland. But a series of severe storms scattered the ships, and the troops never landed. After this incident, the French offered no more aid to the Irish rebels.

The British reacted to the aborted invasion by imposing even tougher restrictions on the Irish. British soldiers confiscated Irish weapons and closed down a radical newspaper in Belfast. Tensions rose and in May 1798, the Irish in many counties joined in rebellion. Tone helped lead the uprising.

At first, the rebels won some victories against the British soldiers stationed in County Wexford near the southeast coast of Ireland. But the British soon received reinforcements under the command of Gen. Gerard Lake. In a savage battle at Vinegar Hill, County Wexford, on June 21, 1798, Lake defeated the rebels. Much of central Ireland then fell into a state of chaos. Both British and Irish soldiers committed cruel and unnecessary acts of violence on innocent victims. British officers turned their backs as their men destroyed Irish crops and massacred thousands of farmers.

More than thirty thousand Irish and British died in the uprising. The victorious British either executed or banished the leaders of the rebellion. In his highly publicized trial, Tone made an impassioned speech demanding freedom for Ireland. Sentenced to death, he asked for the firing squad, the execution accorded to soldiers. The British refused this request and ordered that Tone be hanged on November 12, 1798. That morning, in his cell, Tone cut his own throat with a penknife, thus robbing his captors of their final victory over him.

---

family had only minutes to gather whatever personal belongings they could carry. As the evicted family watched, the agent's hired men tumbled, or tore down, their hut. The agent usually allowed neighbors to take whatever food and furniture existed on the property. In an hour or less, the tumblers reduced the structure to a vacant lot. The agent then ordered other tenants who worked under the landlord to plant wheat, barley, and other profitable crops on the plot.

The evicted family then had no choice but to live in a ditch, a cave, or under the roots of a large tree. Some of those evicted built "scalps," which were holes dug two or three feet deep and covered over with tree limbs and brush. With nothing to eat, few evicted families survived longer than a few weeks or months. One observer said the eviction in Ireland was the same as "a sentence of death by slow torture." Landlords therefore effectively used the threat of eviction to force their tenants to obey their rules.

During the 1700s, Great Britain continued to tighten its grip on Ireland. The penal laws were harshly enforced, and increasing numbers of Irish became poor. The British

Irish revolutionary Theobald Wolfe Tone is captured by British soldiers.

did allow the Irish to have their own legislature, or law-making body, called a parliament. But the Irish parliament was composed solely of Protestants and controlled by the British. Such abuses made most Irish bitter. Anti-British sentiments grew, and many Irish secretly advocated violent revolution.

Tensions mounted until 1798, when the Irish organized a major rebellion. The goal of the uprising was complete freedom from Britain. The British, believing that Ireland was legally a British colony with no right to freedom, met Irish resistance with force. At first, the leaders of the rebellion enlisted the aid of the French. But a fleet of French warships en route to Ireland sank in a series of storms, and the French withdrew, leaving the Irish to face the British alone. In May and June 1798, the rebels fought British soldiers in several bloody battles. The Irish won a few of these engagements, but British reinforcements eventually arrived and cruelly suppressed the uprising. It was the most violent episode in Irish history. The British massacred thousands of Irish peasants, and the total death toll exceeded thirty thousand. The memory of this event remained strong for generations. It made the Irish hesitant about rebelling later, even when the effects of famine and poverty were the most devastating.

Because of the losses suffered on both sides, the British wanted to avoid future rebellions in Ireland. British leaders decided to officially make Ireland a part of Great Britain itself. The Irish would be allowed a few representatives in the British governing body, the parliament. This, argued the British prime minister, William Pitt, would appease the Irish by increasing their economic opportunities. For instance, Pitt believed that if Ireland became a part of Britain, many wealthy British would invest money to modernize Irish agriculture. Called the Act of Union, the merging of Britain and Ireland occurred in 1801.

Another Act of Oppression

The Irish viewed the Act of Union as yet another act of British oppression. In fact, they felt that the union worsened, rather than bettered, their situation. Irish patriots believed the union ruined any future chances for Irish independence. They also felt the union decreased their economic opportunities. The investment of British money in Ireland foreseen by Pitt never happened. Instead, British absentee landlords increased their holdings in Ireland, taking even more of the land away from the Irish themselves. This forced more and more Irish to become poor tenant farmers so that

they could provide food and shelter for their families. For the Irish, the union with Britain dashed their hopes for both self-rule and economic improvement.

Deeper into Poverty

Although most of Ireland sank deeper into poverty after the Act of Union, a few areas of the island continued to prosper. These were the northern port cities, such as Belfast and Derry, through which passed Irish goods bound for Britain. Grains exported included wheat, oats, barley, and rye, the cash crops grown by tenant farmers to pay their rents to British landlords. The Irish also grew wool and cotton. Merchants transported these fibers to the northern port cities. There, a textile industry existed almost solely for the good of the British, for nearly all the cloth produced went to Britain. Most Irish cloth was too expensive for the average Irish peasant to afford.

In other Irish industries, the situation was similar. For example, beer brewing and glassmaking had become small but important industries in Ireland by the late 1700s. In the decades following the 1800 Act of Union, the items produced became specialized to fit the tastes of British consumers. Quality Irish beers could be found only in Britain, while the Irish themselves drank cheap, homemade brews. Beer and glassware, like cloth and grains, left Ireland via the prosperous northern port cities. These centers offered people the only decent,

nonagricultural jobs in the country.

In the early 1800s, Ireland was a land of abject poverty and misery, with the exception of these port cities. The contrast between Ireland and Britain was stark. Only a few dozen miles separated one of the world's richest lands from one of the poorest. Even though they were well aware of the vast inequality of the situation, most British did not think the Irish had been treated unfairly. This was because anti-Catholic, anti-Irish feelings were widespread in Britain. Most British believed Ireland was a crude and uncivilized place. They thought the Irish people were stupid and immoral, capable only of performing menial tasks and producing large families of equally stupid children. Therefore, the Irish were meant to be poor and deserved whatever ills befell them. Such prejudice moti-

vated many British to "keep the Irish in their place," thus perpetuating Irish poverty and misery.

In reality, the plight of the Irish had nothing to do with their intelligence or morals. Most Irish were trapped in conditions of brutal poverty because they were victims of British abuses of their lands and goods. The result was a great mass of poor people, struggling to make a living from the land. All that kept these poor people from death by starvation was the simple potato. This fact would eventually lead to disaster.

Two

A Land Poised on the Brink of Ruin

By the early 1840s, most Irish were poor tenant farmers who had no other means of earning a living. Most farmers grew up on a farm, and farming was the only trade they knew. In fact, many understood how to grow only the particular crops that their families had raised for generations. There were few schools, most of which offered no training in specific job skills, so there was little opportunity for a farmer to learn another trade. Even those rare individuals who knew other trades usually became farmers anyway because there were few nonagricultural jobs available in the country.

Most Irish had little hope that their impoverished way of life would ever change. Armed rebellion seemed out of the question.

After the failed uprising of 1798, the British strengthened their garrisons of soldiers all over Ireland. The presence of these soldiers, along with vivid memories of previous bloodshed, discouraged the peasants from attempting further uprisings. The British controlled the land, the laws, and the courts, and there seemed to be no way for the Irish peasants to escape their poverty.

The deplorable living quarters of the Irish peasants reflected the extent of this poverty. Each farmer constructed a crude hut for his family to live in. These huts were often windowless and fashioned from crude wooden planks covered with mud. There was only one room, and it had a dirt floor. Usually, between eight and sixteen people lived in each hut. More fortunate farmers were able to afford stone cottages with thatched roofs. The huts could be erected in one day, the cottages in two. Furniture was a luxury few could afford. For instance, in 1837, nine thousand inhabitants of a small section of County Donegal owned a total of only 10 beds, 93 chairs, and 243 stools. Most families sat and slept on straw that they spread on the dirt floors. Pigs often slept inside the cabins, and manure piled up in front yards.

Poverty Worsened Effects

Such crushing poverty worsened the effects of two trends that had been developing in Ireland for more than a century. The first was

the people's almost total dependence on the potato as the mainstay of their diet. The second trend was an alarming increase in population. These trends would both have serious consequences.

The Tenant Farmer System

Dependence on the potato developed largely because of the nature of the tenant farmer system. A typical tenant farmer's plot, or holding, consisted of a few acres, although many were a good deal smaller. As a result, the amount of crops that any one family could raise was small. Grain crops like wheat, barley, and oats, which the family used to pay the rent, took up most of the space on a holding. This left little room to grow food for the family to eat. With such limited space, the farmers needed to grow a high-yield crop for food. A high-yield crop is one that produces a large amount of food in a small amount of space. The potato is just such a high-yield crop. On only one-tenth of an acre, a farmer could grow all the potatoes needed to feed a family. This left plenty of space to raise cash crops for the landlord. The tenant farmers found the potato to be very convenient, and they learned to depend on it.

The potato also became popular with Irish farmers because it grows below the ground. Political turmoil, rebellions, and warfare frequently ravaged the countryside. During these times, surface crops like wheat and barley were often

An 1849 etching depicts a mother and son searching for potatoes in a stubble field.

burned or trampled on. But the potatoes, protected by a layer of earth, remained largely unharmed. Thus, the "lumper" or "spud," as the peasants came to call the potato, was always there for the family to eat, even in times of strife.

A Hoe to Turn the Earth

The potato suited the poor Irish in another way. Most of the unskilled peasants lacked the knowledge or money needed to implement advanced farming techni-

22

HOW THE POTATO CAME TO IRELAND

The potato originated as a wild plant in the high plateaus of the Andes Mountains in South America. Primitive Indians learned to cultivate the potato, and later it became a dietary staple of the powerful Inca civilization. Potato fields expanded throughout the breadth of Inca territory, which spanned twenty-six hundred miles. In all, the Incas and later farmers of South America learned to cultivate about four thousand varieties of the potato, which they called *papa*.

In the 1530s, Spanish traders collected samples of papa and shipped them to Europe. At first, the potato was a novelty in Europe. Many feared that the plant had evil properties. People in Scotland refused to eat it because it was not mentioned in the Bible. Some said that eating potatoes would give people diseases like leprosy, consumption, and rickets. But by 1600 many European herbalists, or plant specialists, experimented with the new plant. They found it to be beneficial and began convincing people that potatoes might be an important food source. In the next fifty years, the potato appeared in gardens all over the European continent and on the islands of Britain and Ireland. The Irish were the first Europeans to grow potatoes on a large scale. By the year 1700, the spud was a major crop in Ireland.

ques. It took little skill and practically no money to grow potatoes. All a farmer needed was a hoe to turn the earth during planting. The hoe could also be used to dig up the spuds when they were large enough to harvest. In this way, a farmer could raise potatoes without help. This was fortunate because most Irish tenant farmers were so poor they could not afford to hire farmhands.

Although the potato met many of the needs of the poor, it also had its drawbacks. For one thing, potatoes could not be stored well from season to season like grain. Since farmers planted potatoes in the spring and harvested them in the fall and winter, there were no new spuds in June, July, and August. These became known as the "meal months" because there was always the possibility people would have to resort to eating grain, or meal. Since people would not eat their rent crops, the only way to get meal to eat was to buy it. But the tenants had little or no money. Many resorted to borrowing money from local money lenders. These dealers took advantage of desperate farmers by charging outrageous interest rates. Most people avoided buying meal by rationing their potatoes in hopes of making them stretch over the summer. If the spring crop was lean, those who could not or would not borrow money for meal existed in a state of semi-starvation in the summer.

The most obvious drawback of dependence on the potato was that if the crop failed, there was no other cheap, nutritious food available to replace it. And the potato crop failed often. Between 1816 and 1842, there were fourteen failures. Some failures affected only certain sections of the island. The worst occurred in 1822. Observers reported conditions in the counties of Munster and Connaught as "horrible beyond description." Several thousand people starved to death. To make matters worse, many others could not pay their rents. Some landlords sympathized and did not evict their tenants. But many ordered their agents and local police to evict entire families.

Seasons of rich potato harvests,

A HIGHLY NUTRITIOUS FOOD

Biologists classify the potato under the Latin name *Solanum tuberosum.* An average potato is about 75 percent water. The remainder is referred to as "dry matter." The dry matter contains a great number of ingredients essential to the health of animals and people. One of these ingredients is starch, a carbohydrate that the body converts into energy to power the muscles. Another important component of the potato is protein, which contributes to the growth of body tissues.

Scientists say that potato protein is easily digested and converted to energy by the body. Potatoes also contain many important vitamins and minerals. One potato has half the daily requirement of vitamin C for an average adult. For this reason, people often used potatoes to prevent scurvy, a disease caused by lack of vitamin C.

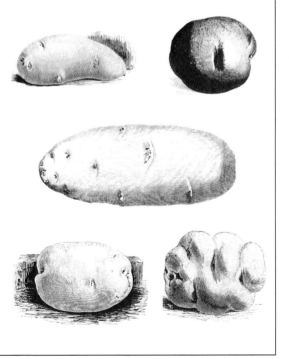

however, followed most lean years. There were even years in which so many potatoes grew that a third of the crop had to be thrown away. The Irish grew accustomed to an unpredictable existence based on the success of the potato crop.

This shaky existence was made even less stable by an alarming population explosion among the Irish poor. Beginning in 1779, the population increased by 172 percent in only six decades, and by 1841 there were at least 8,200,000 people in Ireland. Because the island is so small, the result was an increase in population density, that is, the number of people per unit of space. There was an unusually large num- ber of people crowded into each square mile. In fact, at the time, Ire- land's population density was the highest in the world, greater even than China's. And many historians think even this estimate was too low. Thousands of homeless people were not counted. Some experts estimate that the island's population in the early 1840s was actually between 9 and 10 million people. At least half the people in the country lived in conditions of extreme poverty. Sani- tation was almost nonexistent, and outbreaks of diseases like cholera and typhus were common. Doctors were in short supply, and one medi- cal clinic often served 20,000 people or more.

One reason for the huge population growth in Ireland was religion. Local Catholic priests often emphasized the phrase "Be fruitful and multiply" from the Bible. The Catholic teachings influenced people to raise large families. Most poor Irish couples had at least seven to ten children, and families with twelve to fifteen children were common.

The poor Irish also had many children as the result of cultural influences. Traditionally, parents expected their children to help work the land and tend the farm animals. The more children a couple had, the more help they received. Also, in Irish culture children were expected to support their elderly parents. Parents knew that eventually they would become too old to work and pay the rent. If they were alone, the landlord would automatically evict them. Having many children ensured that someone would be around to take care of them when their productive years were over.

The Poor Married Young

And most of the poor married young. Faced with overcrowded and filthy conditions at home, young people were encouraged to leave and start families of their own. A young couple would strike a deal with a landlord's agent for a plot of their own. No savings were necessary for a down payment because the tenant did not buy the holding. The couple, often with the help of friends, would then build a mud hut on the land. Most people did not have or even expect to have furniture. In the 1830s and 1840s, young Irish people married at an average age of sixteen.

Land Was Scarce

One immediate result of overpopulation in Ireland was a decrease in the size of each tenant farmer's holding, which worsened poverty on the island. Available land was scarce. Almost all fertile land was already owned by absentee British landlords. Although young farming couples could readily acquire holdings from landlords' agents, they never received new farmland. Instead, the agents met the increasing demand for more farms by further subdividing existing plots. All through the early 1800s, farm holdings got smaller and smaller. A four-acre plot became two two-acre plots, then four one-acre plots. Farms on only half an acre were not uncommon. Even on a half-acre farm, the tenant had to find a way to grow enough crops to pay the rent. This became increasingly difficult, and the poor got poorer.

In addition, the farmers themselves often broke up holdings. For example, as a farmer's sons grew to be young men, he might allow them to work part of his holding. Each young man would erect his own hut on his parents' plot and start raising a family. In some cases, as many as ten families would live off one holding. Although this type of subdivision was illegal, often the landlord's agent could be persuaded to keep

quiet about such arrangements. By giving the agent free food, an occasional fat pig, or some other bribe, the farmer made sure the landlord would not find out.

When a landlord did discover that his land had been illegally subdivided, as sometimes happened, the penalties were harsh. The agent almost always evicted the tenant and his family. Most evicted farmers had no job skills, and with few nonfarming jobs available to them, they rarely found other means of support. With no food and no hut, many of the evicted families died of exposure and starvation.

Some evicted people found the strength to migrate to the cities, such as Dublin, located on the eastern coast of the island, or to Belfast and Derry in the north. But the homeless farmers found few opportunities in the urban centers. After the 1800 Act of Union, the cities lost much of their prosperity. Before, these ports traded with many countries. But when Ireland officially became part of Great Britain, trade ended. The port cities became large distribution centers for funneling food and other commodities into Britain. There were not many jobs to be had in these cities, so landless people from the countryside rarely found work. Instead, they huddled in filthy slums, which grew larger and larger during the first half of the nineteenth century. Eventually, the situation for the growing hordes of homeless people was hopeless. They starved both in rural ditches and in city slums.

Ireland in the 1840s was a land

caught up in a cycle of cruel poverty. The conditions suffered by the poor contributed to drastic increases in population. Overpopulation, in turn, greatly increased demands for limited food and land, creating legions of homeless people and still more poverty.

Most of the Irish poor were so preoccupied with day-to-day survival that they were almost totally unaware of events in the rest of the world. Few knew about or took seriously the occasional news stories reporting the failure of potato crops in North America. In 1843 and 1844, potatoes in American fields rotted, stricken by a mysterious disease. The losses were serious but not disastrous, for Americans did not depend solely on the potato as a food source.

The Irish, on the other hand, depended on the potato for their very lives. They had subsisted on spuds for decades and learned to live with the repeated threat of catastrophic mass starvation. It was as if they existed on the brink of a dangerous cliff. No one in Ireland realized that the disease from America would soon arrive and push them over the edge.

Three

A Deadly Blight Brings National Tragedy

In July 1845 Irish farmers had every reason to believe that the soon-to-be-harvested potato crop would be one of the best in years. They inspected their growing potatoes and found them unusually large and plentiful. On July 23, an Irish newspaper, the *Freeman's Journal*, reported, "The poor man's property, the potato crop, was never before so large and at the same time so abundant." On July 25, another paper, the *Times*, announced, "An early and productive harvest is everywhere expected."

But the bountiful harvest never came. The mysterious blight that destroyed potato crops in North America in 1843 and 1844 was on the move. With frightening speed, the disease attacked potato fields in country after country. By August the blight appeared in Holland and France, and in September potatoes in Britain began to die. News of British potato losses quickly reached Ireland, and fearful Irish farmers prayed the pestilence would not descend upon them next.

On September 13, the Irish magazine *Gardener's Chronicle* stopped its presses and printed a special report:

> We stop the Press with great regret to announce that the potato Murrain [blight] has unequivocally declared itself in Ireland. The crops about Dublin are suddenly perishing . . . where will Ireland be in the event of a universal potato rot?

Within a few weeks, the disease spread into the central sections of the island. The potatoes became soft and gave off a putrid odor. Then they decayed into a rotten, slimy mass. The Irish were used to crop failures. But those of the past were caused by climatic factors: too little rain or too much, frosts, and so on. This new episode was entirely different. Perfectly healthy potatoes spoiled and melted away before people's eyes. As the deadly blight swiftly moved from farm to farm, from county to county, a wave of fear swept through the Irish countryside.

Suggestions and Theories

What could be the cause of the plague, people asked? The farmers and peasants had numerous suggestions and theories. Some thought static electricity was the

culprit. Others were sure that puffs of smoke from train locomotives had poisoned the air. This pollution, they said, sank into the ground and choked the spuds. Another explanation claimed that vapors rose from "blind volcanoes" located deep inside the earth. In this explanation, the pollution attacked the lumpers from below. Still another proposal suggested that bird droppings caused the blight. Proponents of this theory could not account for the fact that bird droppings had landed on the island for centuries with no ill effects.

Little Scientific Knowledge

So many theories about the nature of the blight abounded because, at the time, there was little scientific knowledge available to explain the causes of disease. Members of the scientific community scoffed at the farmers' theories but were unable to offer any better explanations. For instance, Dr. John Lindley, a well-known botany professor, believed that the blight came from too much rain. He said the spuds had absorbed so much water that a "wet putrefaction" had taken hold of them. Another plant expert also blamed the weather. He declared that "the season has been so ungenial and the absence of sunshine so remarkable during the last two months that the potatoes have imperfectly ripened." But even the uneducated farmers knew that there had been adverse weather conditions many times in the past. Nothing before had produced such a strange and devastating blight. The sad fact was that no one had a satisfactory explanation for the cause of the disease.

Days Without Food

As the blight raced through Irish fields, people went for days without food. When days of hunger stretched into weeks, many desperate farmers dug up their seed potatoes, small supplies of spuds set aside to plant future crops. To their horror, the farmers found that the plague had reduced their seed potatoes to a sticky rotten heap. After months without food, people began to starve to death. W. E. Forster, a British traveler in Ireland who witnessed the starvation, reported:

> When we entered a village, our first question was, "How many deaths?" "The hunger has been here" was everywhere the cry, and involuntarily we found ourselves regarding this hunger as we should an epidemic, looking on starvation as a disease. In fact, as we went along, our wonder was not that the people died but that they lived. . . . Like a scourge of locusts the hunger daily sweeps over fresh districts, eating up all before it: one class [of people] after another is falling into the same abyss of ruin.

John Mitchel, an Irish patriot, toured the Irish countryside during the winter. He too witnessed the mounting death toll and saw the effects of prolonged hunger on the living. Mitchel said:

> In the depth of winter we travelled to Galway, through the very centre of that fertile island, and saw sights that will never wholly

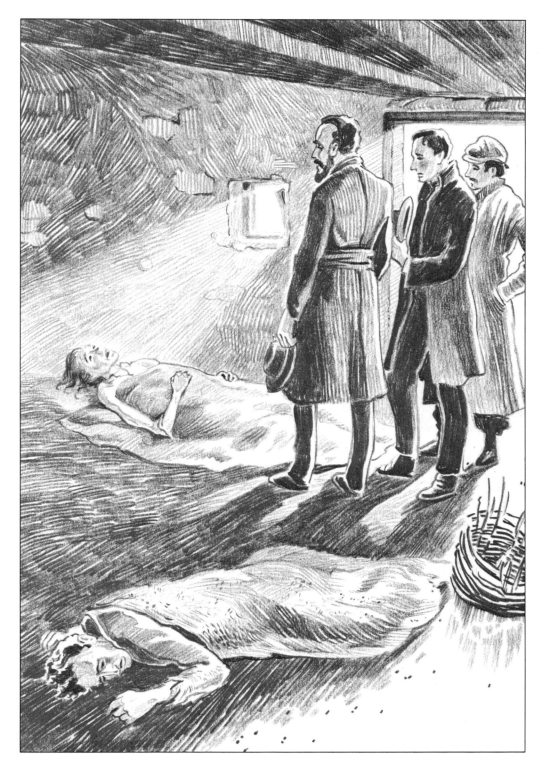

leave the eyes that beheld them—cowering wretches, almost naked in the savage weather, prowling in turnip-fields, and endeavoring to grub up roots . . . sometimes I could see in front of the cottages little children leaning against a fence . . . for they could not stand—their limbs fleshless, their bodies half naked, their faces bloated yet wrinkled, and of a pale greenish hue—children who would never, it was too plain, grow up to be men and women.

In despair, the starving peasants asked what could be done to stop the blight. Was there a way to treat the infected spuds? Dr. Lyon Playfair, a respected chemist, suggested, "It might be possible to mitigate the evil of the potato disease by some chemical application." But he admitted he was not at all sure what chemical should be used. Others proposed salvaging the rotten potatoes. The *Freeman's Journal* called for the building of a machine that would extract the starch from spuds. This starch, the newspaper suggested, might be mixed with flour to make pies and puddings. But no one was sure if it was possible to build such a machine. In any case, health experts pointed out that starch is not the most nutritious ingredient in potatoes. People who lived only on starch would eventually starve to death anyway.

The Plague Raged On

The newspaper the *Nation* printed a recipe for treating diseased potatoes. "Cut off the diseased parts," the recipe instructed, "and steam

An etching depicts a starving boy and girl raking the ground for potatoes.

or boil into a mash with bran and salt." Those who tried this method found it did not work. Other suggested treatments called for soaking the potatoes in bog water or exposing them to poisonous gas. And some advocated baking the spuds until the foul-smelling "blackish matter" oozed out. None of these methods worked. No one knew where the blight came from or how to stop it, and the plague raged on through the countryside.

By the spring of 1846, the Irish peasants were desperate. Some re-

34

sorted to eating diseased potatoes. They became ill and vomited. Fever spread, as did dysentery, an infection of the intestines that causes severe diarrhea. Increasing numbers of tenants even risked punishment or eviction and ate some of their rent crops. The landlords' agents checked these crops often and reported shortages. After eating their rent crops, many poor tenants could not pay their rents. The landlords were well aware that their tenants were suffering. Yet many landlords cared only about making money and cruelly evicted any families that failed to pay rent. As a result, the number of evictions in Ireland increased dramatically during the blight.

During the worst days of the famine, the heartlessness of the landlords caused shameful evictions in every county in Ireland. Witnessing such events, John Mitchel wrote, "Pity and Terror! What a tragedy is here—deeper, darker than any *bloody* tragedy even yet enacted under the sun. . . . Who will compare the fate of men burned at the stake, or cut down in battle . . . with this?" Mitchel said that British landlords and government officials should do something to stop such abuses and help alleviate the misery of the Irish. W. E. Forster agreed, saying that only the British could end the suffering. Ireland, he said, must look "to England . . . to save the lives of her children."

At first, the British government did nothing about the blight in Ireland. Reports about the crisis that reached Britain were often sketchy and contradictory. Most British held the opinion that the situation in Ireland was not all that bad. After all, the Irish had suffered crop

Many Irish attempted to resist eviction, knowing that it meant certain death. Most however, were unsuccessful.

failures before and survived. Many British cautioned against making too much of a fuss over a minor problem. The blight, they said, would go away on its own, and Ireland would be the same as before.

But the British prime minister, Sir Robert Peel, knew better. As early as the fall of 1845, he sent officials to study the problem. They predicted the possibility of a large-scale disaster in Ireland. One official wrote, "Famine must be looked forward to and there will follow, as a natural consequence, as in former years, typhus fever, or some other malignant pestilence." Unlike many British people at the time, Peel was genuinely concerned about the Irish. He believed that since the Act of Union had made Ireland a part of Britain, the Irish should be treated like other British citizens. Peel's opinions about Ireland were unpopular with many British people.

A Substitute Had to Be Found

To save the Irish from starvation, Peel realized that a substitute had to be found for the potato. Shipping large amounts of wheat, barley, and other grains to Ireland seemed the only realistic solution to the problem. But where would the grain come from? The British consumed most of the grain grown in Ireland and Britain. Grain for famine relief would have to come from other countries. But mass importation of foreign grain was forbidden by trade rules called the Corn Laws. Peel decided on a bold

SIR ROBERT PEEL

Sir Robert Peel (1788-1850) was one of the greatest British statesmen of the nineteenth century. He became a member of Parliament in 1809 at the age of twenty-one. Three years later, he received an appointment as chief secretary to Ireland. During the six years he held this office, Peel developed a respect for the Irish people.

Unlike most British leaders, Peel saw conditions in Ireland firsthand. He learned that the crushing poverty was not the fault of the Irish people, which was widely believed in Britain. Instead, he realized that the plight of the Irish was primarily the result of long-standing British political and economic policies. While in Ireland, Peel tried his best to improve the deplorable living conditions of the poor. During the famine of 1817, his tireless efforts to raise money for relief operations for the needy saved thousands of lives.

Many years later, Peel became prime minister of Britain. He held the post twice, from 1834 to 1835 and from 1841 to 1846. During Peel's second term, the potato famine reached its peak. He risked political suicide by calling for the repeal of the Corn Laws. These laws protected British farmers and businesspeople from losing money by blocking imports of cheap foreign food.

Against great opposition, Peel managed to get the Corn Laws repealed in 1846. This made him so unpopular with the wealthy businesspeople in Britain that he had to resign his office on June 29, 1846. But the poor of Britain and Ireland greatly respected him. When Peel died in 1850, there was a huge outpouring of grief by the underprivileged on both islands.

and controversial plan. He would try to convince British lawmakers to repeal the Corn Laws.

The Corn Laws were first established to protect British farmers. The laws placed very high import taxes, called duties, on cheap grain and other foodstuffs from foreign countries. This prevented most foreign grain from entering Britain. As a result, British farmers did not have to compete in the marketplace against the suppliers of cheaper foreign grain. British farmers could keep their prices high and still make large profits. Most people in Britain believed that the strength of the British economy depended on the Corn Laws. They feared that repealing the laws would allow a flood of cheap foreign foods into the country, which, they argued, would cause British farmers to go bankrupt. The economy would collapse, and the social structure of the country would be destroyed. Since Ireland was now a part of Britain, the Corn Laws also applied to grain entering Ireland.

Peel knew that repealing the Corn Laws was a highly emotional issue, one that might ruin his career. But he felt it his duty to try to avoid a catastrophe in Ireland. Courageously, he went ahead with his plans to repeal the laws. He called emergency meetings of the British cabinet and made his case for eliminating the laws. But the other cabinet ministers insisted that repeal would ruin Britain, and they outvoted Peel.

Tens of Thousands Starving

Meanwhile, Lindley and Playfair issued a detailed report of their study of the blight in Ireland. They informed Peel that the situation was dangerous, that tens of thousands of people were already starving. Other eyewitnesses told of seeing entire villages abandoned. John Mitchel called such ghost towns "Places of Skulls" and described returning to a once-prosperous village he had visited two years before.

As Mitchel and his companions approached the town, they saw no animals, no children playing, no smoke rising from the chimneys of the cottages. "There is a horrible silence," Mitchel wrote. "Grass grows before the doors, we fear to look in any door . . . for we fear to see yellow chapless skeletons grinning there." Mitchel did enter some of the houses and, to his horror, found dogs, themselves crazed from hunger, devouring human corpses. As the dogs ran away "with doleful howling," Mitchel and others realized "how *they* had lived, after their masters died." Finding the house of his former host, Mitchel called out a greeting. But there was "no answer—ghastly silence, and a mouldy stench, as from the mouth of burial vaults." Mitchel found the remains of his friends. "They are all dead," he wrote later. "The strong man and the dark-eyed woman, and the little one . . . they shrunk and withered together . . . their horrid eyes scowled on each other with a cannibal glare."

Similar gruesome and heartrending stories continued to reach Robert Peel in London. Agonized with concern, Peel took matters into his own hands. Deciding that the Irish needed grain immediately, he secretly ordered a large shipment of Indian corn from the United States. This food later helped many Irish peasants survive the winter of 1845 and 1846.

Disapproved of Irish

Peel ordered the American corn without getting permission from the head of the British treasury, Charles Edward Trevelyan. In accordance with British law, Trevelyan had the final say over spending of government money. This included funds for famine relief—extra food, clothes, medical supplies, and loans to the poor. The problem was that Trevelyan, like so many other well-to-do British, disapproved of the Irish. And he did

CHARLES EDWARD TREVELYAN

Charles Trevelyan (1807-1886) became head of the British treasury in 1838. He oversaw the Irish relief efforts during the great famine of the 1840s. Like most of the well-to-do British people of his day, Trevelyan disliked the Irish. He considered them to be lazy, vulgar, and stupid.

Trevelyan did not get along with Sir Robert Peel, who served as prime minister when the famine began. The ill will between the two men centered around Peel's open sympathy for the Irish and their plight. All through the famine years, Trevelyan cut back on famine relief programs in order to avoid spending British money on the Irish. He feared more money would make the Irish more dependent on Britain and force his country to drain its treasury.

Even after Peel engineered the repeal of the Corn Laws in 1846, Trevelyan frequently made sure that needed food did not reach Ireland. For instance, on more than one occasion, he saw to it that ships carrying grain from the United States did not dock in Irish ports. Trevelyan even suggested that the ship captains dump their cargoes into the sea. None took his advice. It is certain that Trevelyan's attitude and actions during the famine increased the death toll.

In 1848, Trevelyan profited from the misery of the Irish by publishing a book about his role in the crisis and his travels to Ireland. In the book, titled *The Irish Crisis*, he defended his actions and those of the British government. He also hinted at his personal belief that God had brought the disaster upon the Irish as a form of population control.

not get along with Peel, who wanted to help them. When Trevelyan found out about the shipment of American corn, he was furious.

Trevelyan angrily informed Peel that the British government followed the principles of laissez-faire, an economic theory that holds that the government should stay out of private business affairs as much as possible. According to the theory, a strong economy is a free economy in which individual landowners can buy and sell whatever and whenever they please. Almost every British politician and government official firmly believed in the laissez-faire philosophy and ran the government according to its principles. Trevelyan told Peel that if the government left the landlords and the food distribution system alone, the landlords would feed their own tenants and the famine would end.

British People Disliked Irish

But Peel doubted that many of the landlords would deal fairly with their tenants. He knew that most British people disliked the Irish. The common belief was that too much aid would only make the Irish more lazy and dependent on the British. Many British openly expressed the opinion that an Irish famine might actually be a good thing. Many agreed with the poet Alfred Lord Tennyson, who said about the Irish:

> They live in a horrible island and have no history of their own worth the least notice. Could not anyone blow up that horrible island with dynamite and carry it off in pieces—a long way off?

Peel ran up against such prejudice at every turn, but he continued in 1846 to push for repeal of the Corn Laws.

The Stench of Rotting Spuds

That spring, the Irish potato crop failed again. The stench of the rotting spuds drifted relentlessly across the countryside. Trevelyan's relief efforts were small and poorly managed. He set up a few medical clinics, soup kitchens, and homeless shelters, but they were equipped to serve only a tiny percentage of the hundreds of thousands of sick and starving people. Demonstrations and riots broke out in Ireland.

While people starved, huge quantities of food bound for England left the docks of Belfast and other Irish ports. John Mitchel told how he stood on the docks and wept. "During all the famine years," he wrote, "Ireland was actually producing sufficient food and flax, to feed and clothe not nine, but eighteen millions of people." But British landlords and merchants continued to ship the food and cloth to British markets. Vessel after vessel left Ireland, carrying loads of wheat, oats, cattle, pigs, butter, and eggs.

Mitchel was not the only person to see the food ships departing. Each day, hundreds of starving peasants gathered near the docks and watched helplessly as the food they so desperately needed headed

Although relief efforts were too few and too late, some were organized. Pictured here is a soup kitchen in the county Cork in 1867.

for British dinner tables. Isaac Butt, an Irish politician, described how these impoverished city slum dwellers wandered aimlessly through the streets. They were thin and pale, said Butt, with "emaciated forms. . . . The strong and hale . . . peasant of a few years ago, is now wasted to the weak, and miserable, and half-starved pauper, that sits listless and idle on the flags [stones] of Dublin streets." Both Mitchel and Butt saw the wagons that each morning collected the bodies of those who had died on the streets during the night. The wagons carried the corpses into the countryside for burial in mass graves.

On June 25, 1846, after a fierce political battle, Robert Peel finally managed to push a repeal of the Corn Laws through the British Parliament. But the repeal came too late and did little good. Some foreign grain did reach Ireland. But the flood of goods leaving the island for Britain overshadowed the small amount of relief grain. In a sense, Peel himself now became a casualty of the famine. Angry politicians and adverse public opinion forced him out of office, and the suffering Irish lost their only important British supporter.

Lord John Russell followed Peel as prime minister. Russell did not pressure Trevelyan about relief efforts as Peel had done. So Trevelyan closed down many of the small-scale Irish relief operations he had installed. He did not want the Irish to become too dependent on British aid and bleed the British treasury.

The winter of 1846 and 1847 brought more devastation to Ireland. The justice of the peace of County Cork reported seeing people dying in ditches everywhere. He watched a feverish woman drag the naked corpse of her twelve-year-old daughter to a ravine and cover it with stones. A local doctor found seven people lying in the ruins of a tumbled cottage. One lice-infested cloak covered all seven, one of whom had been dead for several hours. The people were so weak from hunger they could not move.

John Mitchel described how a starving farmer wandered the countryside for weeks, searching for roots and leaves to feed his family. Finally, unable to find the strength to go on, the man went home to die.

Starving Irish rioted against British treatment during the great famine.

DISEASES OF THE GREAT FAMINE

More than one million people died during the great Irish famine. But starvation was not the only cause of death. Disease accounted for nearly half of the toll. Maladies that claimed only a few isolated victims in non-famine years suddenly reached epidemic proportions during the potato blight. The most widespread and serious diseases were typhus, relapsing fever, dysentery, and scurvy.

Typhus and relapsing fever occur when microscopic organisms invade the bloodstream. Typhus begins with headaches, skin rashes, and muscle spasms. The initial symptoms of relapsing fever are severe stomach pain and vomiting. In both diseases, high fevers eventually develop, and the worst cases end in death. During the Irish famine, lice transmitted these diseases to people across the countryside. Unsanitary conditions were common among the Irish poor even in good times. In the famine years, these conditions dramatically worsened. Homeless people often wore lice-infested rags and later passed the filthy garments to other victims. Large families huddled together in caves or around fires, and the lice moved freely from person to person.

Dysentery also spreads fast in unsanitary conditions. This disease occurs when tiny bacteria infect the walls of the intestines. Severe pain and bloody diarrhea are common symptoms. The bacteria eventually pass out of the body in the stools. During the famine, infected human waste littered yards, roadways, and the ditches in which homeless people sought refuge. People rarely washed, and the hungry often ate infected leaves and roots.

Another devastating disease affected the victims—scurvy, which results from a lack of vitamin C. In severe cases, sores appear on the gums, and the teeth loosen and fall out. Blood builds up under the skin, causing black splotches and great pain. Normally, potatoes supplied the Irish with all the vitamin C they required. When the blight removed this important source of the vitamin, scurvy became widespread.

Precise figures do not exist for the numbers of Irish who died from disease during the great famine. At least 250,000 died from typhus and relapsing fever. There were more than 125,000 recorded deaths from dysentery. In all, disease-related deaths during the famine may have exceeded half a million.

Mitchel reported that the man and his wife barely recognized each other: "There is a dull stupid malice in their looks: they forget that they had five children, all dead weeks ago and thrown coffinless into shallow graves . . . and at last, in misty dreams of drivelling idiocy, they die utter strangers."

One Brief Harvest

In 1847, there was one brief harvest of edible potatoes. This fed many people during the winter and offered them hope that the blight was over. But it proved to be a false hope. The pestilence returned stronger than ever in 1848 and 1849. Starvation, disease, and eviction once more took their terrible toll in Ireland.

In the winter of 1849 and 1850, the potato blight finally subsided. But the suffering of the Irish people did not end. In the five years of famine, families were shattered and children orphaned. Over one million people died, and millions more fled the country. And Irish hatred for the British reached a new high. The land known around the world as the beautiful Emerald Isle became a wasteland of desolation and human misery. The famine drained the energies and hopes of the survivors. One Irish woman from County Cork said, "After the famine . . . there was no spirit left in the people."

Four

Death and Flight— Ireland Depopulated

An estimated one and one-half million Irish died of starvation and disease during the great famine. Medical experts estimated that more than half a million people died from disease in the famine years.

There were no official figures for the number of evictions, but contemporary historians believe that they occurred at a rate of about 150 per week. That adds up to more than 38,000 evictions over the five years of famine. In all, at least half a million people lost their homes. Most of these homeless people eventually died of starvation, disease, or exposure to the elements. A majority of the dead were children.

Over the years, much of the blame for this frightening death toll has been placed on the British. Historian Cecil Woodham-Smith said, "The treatment of the Irish people by the British government during the famine has been described as genocide—race murder. The British government has been accused, and not only by the Irish, of wishing to exterminate the Irish people." But, as Woodham-Smith and other scholars point out, the British did not have a specific plan to destroy the Irish.

"It is not characteristic of the English to behave as they behaved in Ireland. As a nation, the English have proved themselves to be capable of generosity, tolerance . . . but not where Ireland is concerned," said Woodham-Smith. There was a prejudice "felt by the English towards the Irish . . . rooted far back in religious and political history." This prejudice, along with a strong belief in the idea of laissez-faire, compelled the British government to neglect the Irish during the great famine.

White Slaves

Much of the suffering of the Irish during the famine was caused by the absentee British landlords. The British Parliament later blamed these wealthy landowners, saying they were "very much like slaveholders with white slaves." One member of Parliament said that the landlords had abused "the great powers entrusted to them by the law." They had brought a "whole people to the

A steady stream of Irish emigrated before, during, and after the years
of the great famine.

brink of starvation . . . the landlords had not done their duty." The government punished many landlords by charging them high fines. Some were imprisoned, and many others suffered public disgrace.

But disciplining some of the landlords did nothing to ease the suffering of the Irish people. In addition to the great numbers who died, many more fled their homeland in search of better living conditions. During the winter of 1847, for example, Irish emigration to other countries increased dramatically. That year, more than 215,000 people embarked for foreign lands from the Irish ports of Sligo, Baltimore, Westport, Killala, and others.

Coffin Ships

The ships leaving these ports were almost always overcrowded. Such vessels did not have adequate food and water to sustain the number of people on board. These dangerous boats became known as "coffin ships." Sometimes, overcrowding caused the bottoms of the vessels to scrape underwater rocks, which could cause a ship to capsize. One ship that sailed from Westport in 1847 sank within sight of the town. Relatives who had just said good-bye to the emigrants watched helplessly as everyone on board the ship drowned.

A typical coffin ship, the *Elizabeth and Sarah,* sailed from Killala to Canada in 1846. The vessel was supposed to carry 12,500 gallons of water but carried only 8,700 gallons. There was not enough food

WHERE IRISH EMIGRANTS WENT

During the years of the potato famine from 1845 to 1850, more than one and one half million Irish fled to other lands. About the same number emigrated in the twenty years that followed, mostly to escape the extreme poverty that persisted in Ireland after the famine. Many of the emigrants went to Britain. In 1841, just prior to the famine, England, Scotland, and Wales had a combined Irish population of some 419,000. In 1851, immediately after the famine, the figure rose to nearly 734,000. The majority of the emigrants chose former British colonies such as Canada, the United States, Australia, and New Zealand as destinations. The Irish reasoned that adjusting to a new culture would be easiest in these lands, where people spoke English and social customs were familiar.

48

for the 276 passengers, who had to share thirty-two sleeping berths. There were no bathrooms or other sanitary facilities on board. One passenger later described the state of the ship as "horrible and disgusting beyond the power of language to describe." During an eight-week voyage, forty-two people died of hunger and thirst. It is estimated that more than five thousand Irish died on the way to other countries during the famine years.

Prejudice and Hatred

Most of the 1847 emigrants went to North America, 110,000 to Canada alone. Unfortunately, these emigrants faced the same prejudice and hatred in their new country that they experienced in Ireland. One reason the Canadians reacted inhospitably was that they feared the Irish would bring disease to Canada. In fact, thousands of Irish suffering from fever and dysentery did arrive in Canadian ports in 1847. On May 31, forty ships lined up on the St. Lawrence River. Many of those on board were sick. They waited for days, even weeks, to get permission from Canadian officials to disembark.

Worried Canadian authorities eventually passed a law that eliminated cheap tickets on ships crossing the Atlantic Ocean. As a result, most of the poorest Irish could not afford the trip and had no choice but to stay in Ireland. Thus, the Canadians accomplished their goal of keeping at least some of the Irish out.

To escape the famine, Irish peas-ants also fled to the United States. In fact, more Irish emigrated to the United States than to any other country. More than 800,000 came in the 1840s. And another 900,000 came in the 1850s. Like the Canadian authorities, U.S. officials were worried about the extreme poverty of the incoming Irish. There was a general feeling that the United States might become "the poorhouse of Europe." People were afraid that the British and other foreigners would try to get rid of their paupers by sending them to the United States. This unreasonable fear caused the U.S. Congress to pass two Passenger Acts in March 1847. These acts reduced by one-third the number of passengers a British ship could carry to the United States. Authorities also greatly increased the price of passage in hopes of discouraging the poor from making the trip.

At first, the Irish had a difficult time living in the United States. Most were afraid to try farming again. So they settled in northeastern cities like Boston, New York, and Philadelphia. Work was hard to find, and most Irish occupied overcrowded, filthy slums. And they constantly had to deal with prejudice. Many Americans feared that Irish Catholics would multiply, overrun the country, and take orders from the Catholic pope in Rome instead of the American president. Anti-Catholic riots rocked New York and other American cities. Often, members of anti-

Irish emigrants pack up their belongings and receive the blessing of the local priest.

Irish organizations and even the police chased and beat up Irish-Americans for no reason.

The Irish Endured

But the Irish endured the abuses they received in the United States. They remembered the terrible conditions they had escaped in Ireland and vowed to succeed in their new homes no matter what the cost. And they worked hard. Irish men labored for low wages building canals and railroads. Many of the women found jobs as housemaids and seamstresses. They saved their money, sending some of it back to Ireland to pay for ship passages for relatives and friends. Eventually, Irish-Americans rose to positions of power in the United States. They became police officers, fire fighters, municipal clerks, politicians, and government officials.

Emigration from Ireland continued throughout the rest of the nineteenth century. By 1890, three million Irish lived in foreign countries, nearly as many as lived in Ireland itself. Of the "overseas" Irish, 84 percent resided in the United States, 8 percent in England, and 7 percent in the British Commonwealth nations of Canada, Australia, and New Zealand. By the early 1900s, there were about four million people living in Ireland.

In addition to population loss through emigration, the potato famine had other long-term effects. Widespread poverty continued in Ireland for generations and re-

"NO IRISH NEED APPLY"—ANTI-IRISH PREJUDICE

About 75 percent of the Irish who emigrated to other lands during the great famine went to the United States. Many Irish believed the United States to be the "home of liberty," a place where downtrodden people had an opportunity for advancement. But the Irish who traveled to America during and immediately after the famine encountered a prejudice much worse than that of the British.

Many Americans saw the poor Irish peasants as shiftless, ignorant, and not "fit for liberty." There was fear among American Protestants that the incoming Irish Catholics were part of a scheme organized by the Catholic pope in Rome. Many Protestants believed that the Catholics, taking their orders from the pope, wanted to take over and control American institutions. In addition to this unreasonable dread of Catholicism, there was the fear that desperate Irish workers would work for cheap wages, take away jobs from Americans, and lower the general level of wages in the country.

Anti-Irish riots erupted in U.S. cities during the late 1840s and early 1850s. The worst period of unrest occurred from 1854 to 1855. Mobs burned Catholic convents and churches and beat and killed innocent Irish-Americans. Few employers hired the Irish for anything but the most menial jobs. And the phrase "no Irish need apply" often appeared on help-wanted signs in the windows of stores and businesses. Because they could not find well-paying jobs, most Irish remained poor. They had to live in dirty, ill-kept slums, where disease, crime, and alcoholism were common. This reinforced the popular stereotype of Irish people as ignorant, drunken bums.

But American anti-Irish bigotry slowly decreased. Many Irish fought with distinction in the Civil War and gained the respect of their fellow soldiers. The Irish also worked hard and saved their money. Many eventually moved from the slums and began to mingle with people in the upper levels of American society. In addition, the Irish adapted well to their surroundings. They quickly learned American customs and business practices, and many Irish rose to positions of power. By 1900, the Irish had become part of the American mainstream.

mains common today. British mistreatment during the crisis left a legacy of deep hatred of the British. Many Irish people could not forget the accusations of Lord John Russell, the British prime minister during most of the famine years. When the potato crop failed in 1848, and the plight of the Irish poor worsened, Russell blamed the Irish themselves. He said the British government had spent great sums of money in 1847 to help the Irish get back on their feet. He insisted that the money had been wasted on the Irish who were lazy and refused to find a replacement for the potato. "How can such people be assisted?" he asked angrily. Many British shared Russell's anti-Irish bias. The mutual dislike of the Irish and British continues into the twentieth century, and much resentment between the two peoples still exists.

Five

World Hunger— Famine Still Plagues Humanity

One of the most frightening aspects of the great Irish famine was the fact that no one, including scientists, knew what caused the deadly potato blight or how to stop it. Although the blight subsided in 1850, it did not go away. In every year since 1850, at least one Irish county reported potato losses caused by the blight. Occasionally, the blight returned on a massive scale. It struck the entire island in 1879, destroying millions of potatoes and causing great human suffering. It was not until the early 1900s that scientists finally discovered what caused the disease.

The potato blight is a fungus known as *Phytophthora infestans,* which is spread by microscopic cells called spores. Wind and water carry the spores from field to field, where they attach themselves to the leaves and other parts of potato plants. Each spore quickly grows into a mass of white tubes that devour the plant. Eventually, the tubes burst open and release thousands of new spores to spread the disease.

Powerless to Stop It

The only effective treatment for the blight is to spray the plants with copper compounds. These slow the growth of the fungus but do not always destroy the spores. Therefore, scientists still do not have a completely foolproof method for eradicating the disease. For this reason, when another large outbreak of *Phytophthora infestans* occurred in Ireland in 1958, people were nearly powerless to stop it from spreading.

The potato fungus also affected other countries over the years. It struck fields in Germany in the 1830s. This led some scientists to suggest that the disease, carried by infected potatoes in the holds of ships, crossed the Atlantic Ocean twice. According to this theory, it first spread from Germany to North America in the 1830s. Later, in the 1840s, the fungus crossed back over to Europe and ravaged Ireland, Belgium, and other countries. The blight struck Belgium again in 1867. A sudden attack on the U.S. crop in 1928 destroyed thirteen million bushels of potatoes in New York state alone. But no outbreak of the blight could be

A starving child during the great Russian famine in 1921. Famine continues
to plague many countries of the world today.

THE CAUSE OF THE POTATO BLIGHT

Many people in the 1840s tried to explain what caused the blight that struck the potato crops of Ireland and other areas of Europe. Various theories blamed the weather, static electricity, volcanic vapors, and bird droppings. No one knew at the time that the real culprit was a fungus called *Phytophthora infestans*. Scientists did not recognize this fungus and correctly explain the way it operates until the early twentieth century.

Phytophthora infestans begins as a small white growth, barely visible to the naked eye, on the exposed leaves of the potato plant. A microscope reveals that the white patch is made up of thousands of tiny strings called fungus tubes. At the end of each tube is a capsule that contains the tiny spores that spread the fungus. The tubes grow quickly, eating away the material of a leaf and its stem.

Eventually, the capsules at the end of the fungus tubes open and the microscopic, cell-like spores escape. Some fall to the ground, and moisture carries them through the soil. There, they attack the tuber of the plant, the potato itself. The tubes multiply again, devouring the cells of the spud. The potato quickly blackens and turns into a foul-smelling pulp.

The wind picks up the other spores released by the fungus capsules. In moist, warm conditions, a diseased plant can give off several million spores. In this way, the spores from a single blighted plant can infect thousands of other plants. The blight can spread over hundreds of square miles in just a few days.

compared in scope and severity to the one that struck Ireland in the 1840s.

Scientists and historians agree that the Irish potato blight was destructive and impossible to stop. Yet these experts say that the disease would have caused much less death and misery if Ireland had not been so overpopulated. They point out that because there were so many people on the island, there was an unusually large demand for food. When the blight destroyed the potato, the main food source, the demand could no longer be met. Even if the British had staged massive relief operations, say the experts, they could not have fed eight million people on a daily basis. If the population of Ireland had been much lower, even modest relief efforts might have kept people from starving to death. The size of the catastrophe that struck Ireland was directly related to the number of people who lived on the island.

Overpopulation a Key Factor

In fact, overpopulation has been a key factor in all the great famines in history. In Ireland, China, India, and Africa, the same tragic story has unfolded. In each land, a poverty-stricken populace depended totally on a few locally grown crops. The population grew until there was barely enough food and the harvest of a single season was all that stood between everyday existence and catastrophe. Inevitably, disaster struck, bringing mass starvation.

This connection between population and famine was first recognized and described by the British economist Thomas Robert Malthus (1766-1834). In his 1798 book, *An Essay on the Principle of Population,* Malthus presented his argument that human population always grows faster than the food supply. According to this view, in good economic times, populations grow quickly. The food supply also increases, but at a much slower pace, so that eventually there is not enough food to go around. Malthus said that when such a food crisis occurs, natural checks, such as disease, famine, and war, work to reduce the excess population. In the case of Ireland, famine and disease brutally stopped the island's population growth.

A tragic example of starvation in the modern world is the situation in Africa. In the late 1960s, famine affected large areas of north central Africa, the region directly south of the Sahara Desert. As in Ireland, decades of overpopulation led to a situation in which millions of people lived constantly at the brink of disaster. As the population increased, people cut down more and more trees for firewood. The loss of vegetation caused massive erosion of topsoil, and fertile areas became barren. Droughts came and huge crop failures followed. By 1972, 250,000 people and 3 1/2 million cattle had died. Conditions improved a bit in the mid-1970s, but the drought returned worse than ever in the 1980s. Lakes and rivers

Thomas Malthus, author of *An Essay on the Principle of Population*

dried up. Lake Chad, a body of water covering ten thousand square miles, lost nearly 90 percent of its area by 1985. Between 1984 and 1985, 2 million Africans died of starvation and disease, half in one country alone—Ethiopia.

Corrupt Officials Stole Goods

Nations around the globe offered food and medical supplies to the African drought victims. Some of this relief got through and saved many lives. But a large percentage of the supplies did not reach the needy. Corrupt local officials stole some of the goods and sold them for profit. Other relief supplies were destroyed during a bloody civil war that raged in the midst of the catastrophe.

Rains returned to the stricken

A starving mother and her children wait for food at an emergency station in a remote village in Ethiopia.

African countries in the late 1980s. But most of the people of the region continue to live on the edge of disaster. One season of serious drought or crop failure could again plunge the area into a nightmare of mass starvation.

Only Rarely Give Away Goods

It may seem odd that so many people can suffer from starvation in a world where enough food is grown to feed everyone. Each year, large agricultural countries like the United States, Canada, and Australia produce much more food than they consume. These countries sell some of their surplus food to nations that have poor harvests. For instance, the United States often sells grain to the Soviet Union. But only rarely do wealthy nations give away their surplus goods to starving peoples.

One reason for this is that getting the food to the people who need it is usually costly. In 1973, for example, U.S. transport planes flew food and medical supplies to victims of the African drought. The planes used one ton of fuel for every ton of supplies they carried. Experts estimated that 500,000 to 1 million tons of food would be needed to relieve the famine for a single year. Therefore, 1 million tons of expensive fuel would also be needed. In addition, there were added costs of shipping the goods by rail or truck from the airstrips to the needy villages. Few other governments were willing to spend the large sums of money required. In

Overpopulation is a problem for many countries. In the case of poor, underdeveloped nations, overpopulation can contribute to famine and starvation.

EFFORTS OF THE UNITED NATIONS TO END HUNGER

The United Nations (UN) often provides hunger relief that individual countries cannot or will not provide. Several UN programs offer aid to famine victims and also work to prevent future famines. The Food and Agriculture Organization (FAO) is a U.N. branch that helps underdeveloped countries improve farmlands, forests, and fisheries. A part of the FAO, the World Food Program (WFP) collects food and cash donated by UN member countries. In times of emergency, the WFP helps distribute such relief.

Another UN program, the World Food Council (WFC), helps developing countries create their own national food strategies. The WFC teaches government officials to calculate how much food they need, where it can be stored, and how it can be transported and distributed during emergencies.

Most experts believe that curbing population growth is the most effective way to prevent future famines. The UN Population Fund (UNPF) sponsors programs that show people in developing countries how to keep their populations from growing too quickly.

addition, some wealthy nations are reluctant to hand over food to corrupt officials who might sell it for personal gain, which happened in Africa. Although some countries do give generously during famines, many victims still go hungry. And as populations rise, the number of victims increases each year.

Is there a way to stop overpopulation? Some experts say that, sooner or later, Malthus's natural checks of famine, disease, and war will decrease the population. But these processes produce widespread destruction and human misery. Malthus himself offered a better solution. In addition to natural checks, he argued that preventive checks should be used. These are methods that reduce the rate of human reproduction. One such check is family planning, the decision of a couple to have fewer children. Another effective preventive check is the use of contraceptives, devices that prevent pregnancy. Population growth in developed countries like the United States has slowed dramatically in recent years due to widespread practices of these methods.

Unfortunately, in developing countries many of the poor are uneducated and unaware of available methods of birth control. Often, their governments cannot afford to institute programs that teach these methods. To help, the United States, the Soviet Union, and other developed countries sponsor such programs in developing countries. The United Nations also runs population prevention programs around the world.

The world is not likely to see an end to devastating famines until all countries overcome two difficult problems. First, a way must be found to quickly ship adequate food and other relief supplies to those who need them. Second, and most important, all countries must learn to curb their population growth. Demographers, scientists who study population patterns, say that if such growth continues unchecked, there will be more than ten billion people in the world by the year 2050. The experts warn that many of these people may suffer the same fate as the Irish in the 1840s. Only when people find a way to manage their own numbers will devastating famines become a thing of the past.

Glossary

coffin ships: old and undersupplied vessels that carried millions of Irish emigrants to other countries

duties: taxes on imported goods

herbalist: a plant expert

high-yield crop: a crop that produces a great deal of food in a small amount of space

laissez faire: the theory that government should stay out of private business. Supposedly, allows free trade to develop on its own and produces a healthy economy

lumper: a nickname for the potato

papa: the name given the potato by the people of South America

parliament: a legislative or lawmaking body in a government, originally in Britain

Phytophthora infestans: the technical name for the fungus that causes the dreaded potato blight

polytheistic: believing in many gods

population density: the amount of people that exist in a given physical space. The more people in the space, the higher the density

ri: a king or chieftain in ancient Celtic times

scalp: a shallow hole in the ground covered with tree branches and brush. Homeless people lived in them during the Irish famine

scurvy: a deficiency disease caused by lack of vitamin C

solanum tuberosum: the technical name for the potato

spud: a nickname for the potato

tuath: a kingdom in ancient Celtic times

tuber: the part of the potato plant that grows beneath the ground, the potato itself

tumbling: the process of evicting a family in nineteenth-century Ireland, in which the family cottage was tumbled, or torn down

Works Consulted

Edwards, R. Dudley and Williams, T. Desmond, editors, *The Great Famine, Studies in Irish History 1845-1852*. New York: Russell & Russell, 1957.

Foster, R. F., *Modern Ireland, 1600-1972*. London: Penguin Press, 1988.

MacManus, Seumas, *The Story of the Irish Race*. New York: Devin-Adair Company, 1921.

Rhoades, Robert E., "The Incredible Potato," *National Geographic*, May 1982.

Ward, Kaari, editor, *Great Disasters: Dramatic True Stories of Nature's Awesome Powers*. Pleasantville, New York: Reader's Digest Association, 1989.

Woodham-Smith, Cecil, *The Great Hunger*. New York: Harper and Row, 1962.

Editors of the Encyclopaedia Britannica, *Disaster! When Nature Strikes Back*. New York: Bantam Books, 1978.

Index

Act of Union, 16
Africa, 55-56

Book of Durrow, 11
Book of Kells, 10, 11
Britain
  Irish imports, 41
  penal laws, 12, 14
  potato famine aid, 36, 39-41, 43, 46, 54
  rebellions against, 14, 15-16, 20
  taxation of Ireland, 12
  treatment of Irish, 18-19, 40, 41, 46, 51
  union with Ireland, 16

Catholic Church
  history, 10, 12
  overpopulation and, 27
  persecution by Britain, 12
  riots against, in U.S., 51
Celts, 8, 10
Corn Laws, 38, 39, 42

diseases, 35, 44
druids, 8
dysentery, 35

emigration of Irish, 50
  difficulties of, 48-49
  to Canada, 49
  to United States, 49, 51
Essay on the Principle of Population, 55
eviction, 13-14, 24, 28, 35

famine
  and overpopulation, 54-55, 58-59
  in Africa, 55-56
  relief efforts, 56, 58
farmers, tenant
  Act of Union and, 16
  crops and, 22
  evictions, 13-14, 24, 28, 35
  jobs and, 20
  land holdings, 22, 27-28
  living conditions, 20-21
  potato and, 22-25
  poverty, 12-13, 19, 20
Food and Agriculture Organization, 58

Forster, W. E., 32, 35
France, 14, 15

illuminated manuscripts, 10, 11
Ireland
  history
    British rule, 8, 12, 19
    Catholic Church, 10, 12
    Celts, 8, 10
    Protestant Church, 12
    rebellion of 1798, 14, 15-16
    union with Britain, 16
  industries, 16
  Parliament, 15
  poverty, 13, 19, 25, 51
    diseases and, 25
    in cities, 28, 42
    overpopulation and, 25, 27, 29
  religion, 8, 10, 12
  starvation in, 24, 32, 34, 38, 39, 42
    and exports to Britain, 41
Irish
  anti-British feelings of, 12, 15, 45, 51
  farmers, 12-13, 16, 20
  emigration of, 48-50
  geography, 8, 10

King Henry VIII, 12

laissez-faire, 41
Latin language, 10
laws
  Corn Laws, 38-39, 42
  Passenger Acts (U.S.), 49
  penal, 12, 14
Lindley, John, 32, 39

Malthus, Thomas, 55
Mitchel, John, 32, 35, 39, 41, 43, 44

Passenger Acts (U.S.), 49
Peel, Robert, 36, 39, 40, 42
Playfair, Lyon, 34, 39
Pope Adrian IV, 10
potato
  failures, 24-25, 30
    causes, 30, 32, 52, 54

in Germany, 52
in North America, 29, 52
treatments, 34-35, 52
famine, 32, 34, 39, 43-44
and disease, 35, 44
and emigration, 48-50
and evictions, 35, 46
and overpopulation, 54
British aid, 36, 39-41, 43, 46, 54
death toll, 46
end, 44
in cities, 42
landlord responsibility, 46, 48
relief corn, 39, 41
relief grains, 38, 40
history of, 23
Irish dependence on, 22-24
nutritional value, 24
Protestant Church, 12

Russell, John, 43, 51

Saint Patrick, 10
scurvy, 44

taxation, 12
Tennyson, Alfred Lord, 41
Tone, Theobald Wolfe, 14
Trevelyan, Charles, 39-41, 43
typhus, 44

United Nations Population Fund, 58
United States
famine aid
Africa, 56
Ireland, 39, 41
Irish immigrants in, 49-50
potato failure in, 29, 52

Vinegar Hill, battle of, 14

World Food Council, 58
World Food Program, 58

Picture Credits

About the Author and Illustrator

The Author, Don Nardo, is a professional free-lance writer. He has also worked before or behind the camera in twenty films. Several of his musical compositions, including a young person's version of H.G. Wells's *The War of the Worlds,* have been played by regional orchestras. Mr. Nardo's writing credits include short stories, articles, textbooks, screenplays, and several teleplays, including an episode of ABC's "Spenser: For Hire." In addition, his screenplay *The Bet* won an award from the Massachusetts Artists Foundation. Mr. Nardo lives with his wife and son on Cape Cod, Massachusetts.

The Illustrator, Brian McGovern, 35, has been active in both fine art and commercial illustration for twenty years. His recent clients include AT&T, DuPont, Harvey's Lake Tahoe, and Chase Manhattan Bank. He has exhibited paintings in San Francisco and New York and was recently a published winner in *American Artists Magazine* in the "Preserving Our National Wilderness" competition. He has won several Best of Show awards in the fantasy art field and the 1987 Distinguished Leadership Award from American Biographical Institute in North Carolina.